JOHANNESBURG TRAVEL GUIDE 2023:

Discovering Johannesburg's hidden gems with practical tips and safety

By

Dave C. Albert

Table of contents

Introduction to Johannesburg

Johannesburg's Neighbourhood and cuisine

Getting to know Johannesburg's history

Johannesburg's famous places and attractions

Johannesburg's Cultural Scene

Outdoor Adventures in Johannesburg

Shopping in Johannesburg

Johannesburg's Accommodation Options

Transportation in the City

Going beyond Johannesburg

Chapter 1

Introduction to Johannesburg

Johannesburg's Overview

Johannesburg, sometimes known as "Jo'burg" or simply "Joburg," is a magnificent metropolis that perfectly captures the vivacious essence of South

Africa. Johannesburg, which is located in the northeast of the nation, is not only the biggest city in South Africa but also one of the most important in terms of the continent's economy and culture. It is a wonderfully intriguing and dynamic city to visit because of its expansive metropolitan environment, rich history, and varied people.

The city of Johannesburg has seen tremendous development throughout the years, which is one of its distinguishing features. As a result of the discovery of gold in the Witwatersrand Basin in the late 19th century, it grew from a modest mining community to a huge city that is today the engine of South Africa's economy. The gold rush period, which drew fortune seekers from all over the world and gave rise to a robust mining sector, is responsible for the city's expansion. With historical sites like the Apartheid Museum and Gold Reef City providing context for the present, this historical relevance is still clear today.

But Johannesburg is a city that always looks to the future; it isn't simply about its past. It has a vibrant arts and cultural scene with a large population of performers, musicians, and artists. One area that stands out as a creative hotspot with galleries, shops, and hipster cafés is the Maboneng Precinct. The city's diverse neighborhoods, which range from the African townships to the affluent areas of Sandton and Rosebank, also exhibit the city's cultural variety.

The economic impact of Johannesburg goes well beyond its limits. It functions as the center of the African continent's economy, including that of South Africa. The Johannesburg Stock Exchange, one of the biggest in the world, is located in the city and attracts investors, businesspeople, and global organizations. This vitality in the economy has given it the moniker "Africa's financial capital."

The skyline of the city, which is dominated by skyscrapers, is a monument to its modernity. Just a handful of the city's many notable buildings are the Hillbrow Tower, the Carlton Center, and the Ponte City Apartments. Nevertheless, despite its modernity, Johannesburg has managed to retain green areas like the Johannesburg Botanical Garden and the Walter Sisulu National Botanical Garden, offering locals and guests tranquil places in order to make your stay enjoyable.

Johannesburg is a city filled with tensions and contrasts. Luxury retail centers and crowded street markets coexist there, where ancient African practices and modern lives mingle in perfect harmony. It is a city that has had a number of difficulties, including the aftereffects of apartheid and persisting social inequalities. But it's also a city that keeps reinventing itself, working to advance and be inclusive.

Finally, it should be noted that Johannesburg is more than simply a city; it is a vibrant, ever-evolving metropolis that embodies the very essence of South Africa. From its historical beginnings in the gold rush to its current position as a major economic force on the world stage, Johannesburg never ceases to enthrall and inspire with its vitality, variety, and resiliency. Johannesburg provides a diverse experience that has a lasting effect on anybody lucky enough to come, whether you're exploring its cultural attractions, doing business, or just taking in the daily life of its lively neighborhoods.

Culture and history

Johannesburg's history and culture are intricately woven together, producing a tapestry that represents both the city's illustrious past and its varied present. We must explore this city's interesting history if we want to understand it fully.

Historical Foundations:

The Witwatersrand Basin's discovery of gold in the late 19th century, which led to a gold rush that completely changed the area, is where Johannesburg's narrative starts. A mining community, first known as Ferreira's Camp, was founded as a result of the influx of prospectors and those looking for their big break. This little community quickly expanded into a thriving metropolis, which was given the new name Johannesburg in recognition of Johannes Meyer and Johannes Rissik, the two men who made the first gold discovery in the region. A varied population was drawn to the area during the gold rush, including immigrants from Europe, Africa, and Asia, which helped to create the city's cosmopolitan culture.

Apartheid Period:
With the establishment of apartheid, a system of racial segregation and discrimination imposed by the South African government, a dark chapter in Johannesburg's history was added in the middle of the 20th century. The city was severely segregated during this time, with black citizens being forcefully relocated to townships like Soweto and Sophiatown. The Apartheid Museum, a somber tribute to the fight for freedom and equality, has remains of this period that may be visited. Apartheid left permanent wounds in the city's geography and mental makeup.

Diversity of Culture:
The richness of Johannesburg's culture makes it flourish. The city is a linguistic, cultural, and culinary melting pot. You may see a confluence of cultures via art, music, and cuisine in its energetic areas, including Melville, Maboneng,

and Fordsburg. The vibrant music culture in the city embraces everything from jazz and hip-hop to traditional African rhythms, while its street markets, like the Neighbourgoods Market, provide a sensory voyage through various tastes.

Creativity and the Arts:

Gauteng is a center for creative expression. Numerous theaters, art galleries, and the Market Theatre—which was instrumental in the fight against apartheid—can be found in the Newtown Cultural Precinct. Galleries like the Everard Read Gallery and the Goodman Gallery, which present the work of both renowned and up-and-coming artists, are thriving centers for contemporary South African art.

Cultural Celebrations:

Every year, a variety of cultural events animate the city. One of the most important cultural events in South Africa is the National Arts Festival in Makhanda (formerly Grahamstown), which showcases theater, music, and visual arts. The Joy of Jazz Festival and the Soweto Wine and Lifestyle Festival are just two examples of Johannesburg's rich cultural calendar.

Sports and History:

An important part of Johannesburg's culture is sports. The city is home to renowned venues, including Soccer City's FNB Stadium, which served as the site of the 2010 FIFA World Cup final. Rugby, cricket, and football are popular activities that bridge ethnic and class divisions, and Johannesburg has a rich athletic history.

In essence, Johannesburg's history and culture are examples of adaptability and change. This city has consistently changed, from its modest beginnings during the gold rush through its turbulent apartheid years to its current standing as a dynamic, multicultural metropolis. It invites people who come to South Africa to discover its fascinating past and embrace its colorful culture as a symbol of the country's development towards unification, diversity, and growth.

Location and climate

The biggest city in South Africa and the provincial capital of Gauteng, Johannesburg, is not only a humming economic center but is also distinguished by its particular climate and location. Let's take a closer look at Johannesburg's topography and climate to understand what makes it unique.

Location in the world:
Johannesburg is ideally placed on the Highveld plateau in northeastern South Africa. This plateau, which rises to a height of around 1,753 meters (5,751 feet) above sea level, gives the city a number of distinctive features. Due to its proximity to South Africa's geographic center, Johannesburg plays a significant role in the nation's transportation and economy.

Landscapes and Environments:
There are many different types of scenery all around the city. The gorgeous Magaliesberg Mountains, which are located to the north and west of the city and provide options for outdoor

recreation, are a beautiful background for the area. In the east, the topography gets more undulating as it approaches the lowveld districts of Mpumalanga and Limpopo, while in the south, the environment gradually changes into the highveld's lush plains.

Overview of the climate:
Highland or subtropical highland climate is a common description of Johannesburg's climate. It has four very different seasons:

1. Summer in Johannesburg lasts from December to February, and average temperatures range from 15°C (59°F) to 25°C (77°F). However, during hot periods, it's not unusual for temperatures to rise beyond 30°C (86°F). In addition to being wet, summer is also a thunderstorm-prone season.

2. Autumn (March to May): Daytime highs in the autumn range from 15 to 24 degrees Celsius (59 to 75 degrees Fahrenheit). As there is less rain in the city, this is a good time to travel.

3. Summer (November to May): Summers in Johannesburg are warm during the day and chilly at night. While nighttime lows may reach 4°C (39°F), daytime temperatures typically range from 16°C (61°F) to 20°C (68°F). There is little to no rainfall throughout this dry season.

4. During spring (September to November), temperatures rise, with highs between 17°C (63°F) and 26°C (79°F). The city begins to blossom with colorful flowers and vegetation during this transitional season, which has good weather.

Influence of Altitude and Climate:
The climate of Johannesburg is substantially impacted by its high height. In comparison to other South African cities, the city has lower humidity levels and more moderate temperatures because of its height. Additionally, it indicates that Johannesburg is less vulnerable to illnesses like malaria, which are more common in warmer, lower-lying areas of the nation.

In conclusion, Johannesburg has a distinct climate that is brought about by its position on the Highveld plateau, surrounded by a variety of landscapes, and its height of almost 1,700 meters (5,500 feet) above sea level. Understanding the city's climate and location is essential to getting the most of your time in Johannesburg, whether you're taking in the city's thriving cultural scene, doing business in its commercial district, or just taking in its unique natural beauty.

Methods of transportation

With a range of options for transportation, reaching Johannesburg, the thriving economic and cultural center of South Africa, is an exhilarating adventure. Being a significant global center, the city is easily accessible from anywhere on the globe. Let's explore the many routes you might use to get to this fascinating city.

1. By Air:
International Flights: Outside of Johannesburg,

O.R. Tambo International Airport is the busiest airport in Africa and a key entry point to the continent. With various airlines providing direct connections to Johannesburg, it welcomes flights from all over the globe. Shuttle services, taxis, and the Gautrain, a fast train that connects the airport to different areas of Johannesburg, are all convenient ways for visitors to get to the city center.

Domestic Flights: Domestic flights to Johannesburg are an option if you're already in South Africa. Another airport servicing the city is Lanseria International Airport, which largely handles domestic travel but also provides certain regional connections.

2. On the Road:
- Driving: Johannesburg is well connected to other major cities and areas by an extensive network of roads, making it ideal for travelers touring South Africa by car. For instance, the N1 and N3 freeways connect Johannesburg to Cape Town and Durban, respectively. The journey gives an opportunity to explore the country's

many landscapes, from the Highveld's undulating hills to KwaZulu-Natal's lush valleys.

Inter-city Buses: From other South African cities, long-distance buses are an easy and affordable way to get to Johannesburg. Reputable bus companies provide pleasant journeys with a range of facilities, giving passengers a good option.

3. Using the Train:

Gautrain: Johannesburg's cutting-edge and effective commuter rail system, the Gautrain, links the city to Pretoria and the airport and offers a convenient way of transit. It is a convenient and secure method of getting through the city and its surroundings.

4. By bus and coach:

Inter-city Coaches: A number of coach operators provide routes from surrounding nations, including Mozambique, Zimbabwe, and Botswana, to Johannesburg. Even though these trips might be lengthy, they are an economical way to get to the city.

5. From Cruise:

Although it is uncommon for cruise ship passengers to arrive in Johannesburg directly, those who arrive at Durban or Cape Town might opt to extend their trip inland to visit the city. To make things easier, tour packages and transportation are often offered.

6. Using International Rail:

Rovos Rail: Rovos Rail is a luxury train service that provides trips to Johannesburg from towns like Cape Town and Durban. It offers a really exceptional and opulent travel experience. This is a great opportunity to take in South Africa's beautiful surroundings while taking advantage of first-rate facilities and service.

In conclusion, one of Johannesburg's advantages is that it is easily accessible, with a wide range of alternatives available to visitors visiting from both local and foreign regions. Getting to Johannesburg is the first step in exploring the vibrant culture, history, and energy of this wonderful city in the center of South Africa, whether you like the ease of air travel, the excitement of a road trip, or the comfort of a luxury train ride.

Safe practices and advice

Like visiting any large city, traveling to Johannesburg has its own particular experiences and concerns. Despite the city's abundance of attractions and cultural diversity, a smooth and pleasurable stay may be guaranteed by being aware of practical advice and safety precautions.

Here is a thorough guide for visitors visiting Johannesburg:

1. Safety precautions:

You need to stay informed: Before you visit, learn about Johannesburg's current safety condition and review any government-issued travel warnings. Even though the city has considerably improved over the years, certain regions could have greater crime rates.

Neighborhood Awareness: There are many different neighborhoods in Johannesburg, some of which are safer than others. The majority of the time, travelers may feel comfortable visiting places like Sandton, Rosebank, and Melville. Always seek information about safe locations and places to avoid from locals or hotel personnel.

Stay Alert: Be cautious and aware of your surroundings, just as you would in any large metropolis. Keep an eye on your possessions, and keep pricey jewelry and devices hidden if possible.

Avoid Night Travel: You should keep your nighttime travel to a minimum, particularly in uncharted territory. Consider eating and entertainment alternatives that are near your lodging and use reliable transportation.

Use reliable transportation. When getting around the city, use licensed taxis, ride-sharing services, or the Gautrain (the city's commuter train system). Steer clear of unregistered or illegal cabs.

2. Health and security:

Vaccinations: Before flying to South Africa, ask your doctor about the necessary shots. Make sure you are up to date on standard immunizations such as MMR (measles, mumps, and rubella).

Water: Although Johannesburg's tap water is often safe to drink, some tourists prefer bottled water. To keep hydrated, always have a reusable water bottle with you, particularly in the warmer months.

Healthcare: Although Johannesburg boasts first-rate medical services, it is advisable to obtain comprehensive travel insurance that includes medical emergencies.

3. Local customs and protocol:

Respect Cultural Diversity: South Africa is a multicultural country with many different languages and traditions. Be respectful of regional traditions, dialects, and customs while also being curious to learn more about the country's rich history.

Tipping: In South Africa, tipping is usual. It's customary to tip between 10% and 15% of the total cost at restaurants. Whenever appropriate, provide tips to taxi drivers, tour guides, and hotel employees.

4. Connectivity and Communication:

SIM Cards: To ensure dependable and affordable communication throughout your visit, get a local SIM card at the airport or any retailer that sells cell carrier equipment.

Emergency Numbers: Learn the local emergency phone numbers, such as 10111 for the police and 10177 for medical issues.

5. Currency and Money:

The main money spent in South Africa is The South African Rand (ZAR). Although most establishments in Johannesburg accept credit cards, it's still a good idea to have some cash on hand for smaller transactions and in case you visit any locations that don't.

ATMs: There are plenty of ATMs located across the city. Use ATMs that are well-lit and safe, especially inside bank buildings.

6. Weather conditions and packing:

Although Johannesburg has a moderate temperature, the weather may be erratic. Before you pack, check the weather forecast and pack the right clothes for the weather, including sunscreen and a hat.

7. Cultural Attractions include: Plan Ahead: Johannesburg is home to a variety of museums,

galleries, and other cultural attractions. Plan your trips throughout the day and confirm the hours of operation in advance.

You may have a memorable and secure time while discovering Johannesburg's rich culture, history, and energetic environment by being educated and using reasonable care. With the right planning, you may thoroughly enjoy your trip to this vibrant South African city, which has a lot to offer.

Chapter 2

Johannesburg's Neighbourhood and cuisine

Exploring Johannesburg's Neighborhoods

Johannesburg, which is also known as the "City of Gold," is a thriving and diversified city in South Africa. It is well-known for its extensive history, cultural variety, and myriad of neighborhoods, each of which offers its own taste of life. Let's walk casually around some of Johannesburg's most fascinating districts.

1. Sandton: This wealthy neighborhood, which is known for its cutting-edge buildings, opulent retail centers like Sandton City, and a bustling business scene, serves as Johannesburg's economic center. It is a representation of urban

affluence since it is where the financial elite of the city congregates.

2. Maboneng: Maboneng is the place to go if you're looking for art, creativity, and a hipster feel. This gentrified area is a refuge for artists, with streets covered with graffiti, art galleries, and hipster coffee shops. For foodies, The Market on Main is a must-see.

3. Soweto: Soweto, also known as the South West Townships, is rich in both history and culture. It was essential in the fight against apartheid. Visit the old residences of Desmond Tutu and Nelson Mandela to learn more about this nation's turbulent history.

4. Melville: This artistic district has a relaxed appeal. 7th Street in Melville is well known for its thriving nightlife, which includes a wide variety of pubs, eateries, and live music venues. Students and creative types in the city frequent there often.

5. Rosebank: Rosebank is a hip urban district well-known for its food, entertainment, and retail opportunities. Unique handmade items may be found in abundance at the African Craft Market, while the rooftop bars provide breathtaking views of the metropolitan skyline.

6. Braamfontein: The University of the Witwatersrand is located in this bustling center of culture and learning, which also has a wide variety of theaters, art galleries, and street art. It's a vibrant community that's always changing.

7. Kensington: Kensington provides tree-lined lanes, historic houses, and a feeling of community if you're looking for a more sedate, residential atmosphere. It is a tranquil sanctuary within the busy metropolis.

8. Norwood: With restaurants providing food from all around the globe, Norwood is well known for its diversified culinary scene. It is a culinary heaven since it is a mashup of cultures and tastes.

9. Newtown: This cultural district serves as a demonstration of Johannesburg's dedication to the arts. The Market Theatre and Museum Africa, which honor the cultural legacy of the city, are located in the Newtown Cultural Precinct.

10. Fourways: Known for its welcoming ambiance for families, Fourways provides roomy suburban living, malls, including Fourways Mall, and outdoor pursuits. It's a terrific location for anyone looking for peace and quiet while still being close to the city.

Each of these communities adds to Johannesburg's dynamic tapestry by providing something special to locals and tourists alike. Johannesburg's districts offer something to capture everyone's heart, whether you're exploring the ancient streets of Soweto, enjoying international food in Norwood, or soaking in the creative energy of Maboneng.

Regional Food and Dining

You're in for a treat when it comes to Johannesburg's regional food and eating options, which represent the city's rich history, cultural variety, and role as a culinary melting pot. Let's take a savory tour of some of Johannesburg's top eating destinations.

1. Traditional South African Cuisine: You must start your gastronomic tour of Johannesburg with a taste of traditional South African food. "Braai," a barbeque with scrumptious meats like boerewors (sausage) and sosaties (kebabs), is the national meal. Visit a "shisa nyama" location for a genuine local experience, where you can watch your meat being perfectly grilled while taking in the vibrant ambiance.

2. Bunny Chow: Originally from Durban, this delicacy is only found in South Africa, although it has now spread to Johannesburg. It consists of a loaf of bread that has been hollowed out and is then filled with curries, a savory comfort meal

that is also substantial. Many restaurants give their own unique takes on this traditional dish.

3. Pap & Vleis: Pap is a maize porridge often eaten with "vleis" (meat) and a savory tomato-based sauce. It is a mainstay in many South African homes. It's a filling meal that highlights the contribution of regional foods.

4. Bobotie: This is an egg-based meal with savory, seasoned minced beef. It is a mix of tastes from Cape Malay, Dutch, and Indonesian cuisines, and it illustrates South Africa's rich cultural past.

5. Vetkoek: Deep-fried dough balls are a popular South African street dish. They may be filled with a variety of savory or sweet ingredients, such as curry mince, syrup, or jam. Johannesburg is home to many vetkoek sellers, particularly in neighborhood markets.

6. International Cuisines: Due to its diversified population, Johannesburg now offers a wide variety of international cuisines. You may

sample anything from Lebanese mezze to Ethiopian injera, giving you access to a variety of world cuisines.

7. Markets that are alive: The city is peppered with lively food markets, including Rosebank Sunday Market and Neighbourgoods Market in Braamfontein. With their extensive selection of handcrafted goods, vibrant ambiance, and gastronomic treats, these markets are a foodie's heaven.

8. Fine Dining: There is a vibrant fine dining scene in Johannesburg. Numerous award-winning restaurants can be found around the city, where renowned chefs create creative meals that combine regional ingredients with global culinary trends. These places provide a classy and refined eating experience.

9. Craft Beer Culture: Johannesburg has enthusiastically embraced the craft beer revolution. There are more and more craft beer pubs and microbreweries where you may try

locally made beer, often combined with delectable cuisine.

10. Rooftop Dining: Johannesburg has a number of rooftop pubs and restaurants where you may have a meal while taking in the view. The panoramic views of the metropolis provide a spectacular backdrop for any event while you enjoy your dinner.

In Johannesburg, eating is a cultural experience that represents the city's dynamic and changing character. It is not only about the cuisine. Johannesburg's food sector is a monument to the city's dynamic character and the blend of cultures that make it so distinctive, from the street sellers selling traditional favorites to the high-end restaurants pushing culinary frontiers. Therefore, Johannesburg's eating alternatives will satisfy your appetite and leave you wanting more, whether you're a culinary aficionado or just trying new cuisines.

Johannesburg's top restaurants

Johannesburg has a flourishing restaurant scene, with a variety of eateries to suit different tastes and preferences. Let's take a culinary tour of some of the top eateries in this exciting South African metropolis.

1. Located in the center of Johannesburg, Marble is a hidden culinary treasure known for its wood-fired fare. A cuisine created by renowned chef David Higgs honors South African tastes while combining influences from across the world. The restaurant offers a distinctive eating experience thanks to its eye-catching design and open cooking concept.

2. DW Eleven–13: This Michelin-starred restaurant provides a modern dining experience with an emphasis on locally produced, in-season cuisine. Innovative tasting menus from Chef Marthinus Ferreira and well-chosen wine pairings make for an unforgettable gastronomic experience.

3. The Test Kitchen: Despite having its roots in Cape Town, this famed pop-up restaurant sometimes makes an appearance in Johannesburg. With a multi-course tasting menu that pushes the frontiers of South African cuisine, it routinely ranks among the best restaurants in the nation.

4. Mosaic at the Orient: This superb dining establishment is located in the serene surroundings of the Orient Boutique Hotel. The restaurant's lovely garden contributes to the mood, while chef Chantel Dartnall crafts wonderful meals using natural ingredients as inspiration.

5. The Grillhouse is a well-known institution among fans of traditional cuisine and flawlessly cooked steaks. This well-known eatery has been serving premium meat for many years and has a sizable wine selection to go with your meal.

6. Farro: Located in Illovo, Farro is a modern Italian eatery with a solid reputation for its tasty and fresh food. It's a favorite among fans of

Italian food, serving everything from handmade pasta to wood-fired pizza.

7. La Colombe: Despite being a Cape Town institution, La Colombe's Johannesburg location offers the city its renowned fine dining experience. The eatery has an outstanding tasting menu that highlights Chef James Gaag's inventive cooking.

8. Urbanologi: Situated in the buzzing 1 Fox Precinct, Urbanologi blends South African and Asian cuisines. Innovative small dishes, artisan beers, and an industrial-chic atmosphere combine on the menu, making this a popular location for beer and cuisine lovers.

9. The Fat Zebra: Located in Linden, this little eatery is renowned for its seasonal menu changes and dedication to using locally produced foods. Locals love it because of the welcoming ambiance and excellent service.

10. Rockets: Rockets is more than simply a restaurant; it's a chic gathering place. It's a place

to be seen while having dinner with friends because of its contemporary design, broad drink menu, and different culinary selections.

Restaurants in Johannesburg provide everything from modern South African cuisine to foreign cuisines offered in a variety of settings, which is a monument to the city's multicultural heritage. These finest restaurants in Johannesburg guarantee a pleasurable and unforgettable dining experience, whether you're looking for a romantic supper, a gourmet adventure, or a casual lunch with friends. Keep in mind to book reservations in advance since these restaurants are often busy. Take pleasure in your culinary tour of the "City of Gold"!

Entertainment and Nightlife

As the sun sets over Johannesburg's expansive metropolis, a thriving and exhilarating nightlife scene comes to life. Johannesburg provides a wide variety of entertainment alternatives to suit every taste and desire, from energetic nightclubs to warm jazz bars and everything in between. Let's explore this South African city's vibrant nightlife and entertainment scene.

1. Johannesburg is well known for its nightlife, and the city is home to a wide variety of top-notch nightclubs that keep the party going until the wee hours of the morning. Famous clubs like Taboo, Kong, and The Sands often attract famous DJs from across the world, drawing partygoers from all around the city. Expect to dance in elegant venues to the newest tunes.

2. Jazz & Live Music: Johannesburg's jazz culture is unmatched for those who seek a more relaxed and soulful experience. Live jazz concerts by both up-and-coming musicians and seasoned performers are often held at places like The Orbit and The Bassline. It's an opportunity to enjoy the soothing sounds of South African jazz in a cozy environment.

3. Cocktail Bars: Johannesburg has a wide selection of upscale cocktail bars if you're in the

mood for handmade drinks and fashionable environs. Try Marble for rooftop views and creative concoctions, Sin + Tax for masterfully made cocktails, or Sinns Restaurant and Lounge for an elegant evening of mixology.

4. Laughter is a global language, and Johannesburg's comedy clubs are sure to make you smile. Local and international comedians may be seen at places like The Goliath Comedy Club and Parkers Comedy and Jive, which provide a fun night out.

5. Theatre and performing arts: The performing arts are a part of Johannesburg's cultural landscape. While the Joburg Theatre presents a range of acts, from musicals to ballet, the Market Theatre is a center for cutting-edge theatrical productions. These places give visitors a flavor of the aesthetic diversity of the area.

6. Explore Johannesburg's vibrant art galleries for a more elegant evening. There are several galleries in the Maboneng Precinct that display the creations of gifted local artists. It's an

opportunity to fully experience the city's modern art scene.

7. Breweries and Craft Beer: Johannesburg is a sanctuary for craft beer lovers. Craft breweries and taprooms have proliferated in the city, including Mad Giant and Black Horse Brewery, which provide a casual venue to try uncommon beers.

8. Casino entertainment is available in the Fourways suburb's Montecasino, which also has a variety of restaurants, theaters, and entertainment centers. It is a one-stop shop for an exciting night out.

9. Experience South African culture by attending traditional dance performances or visiting cultural centers like Lesedi Cultural Village, where you can learn about and take part in the traditions of the many South African ethnic groups.

10. After a night of celebration, Johannesburg's late-night restaurants come to the rescue. Visit

restaurants like Dino's, the Radium Beer Hall, or The Rock for robust meals to satiate your post-party desires.

The nightlife and entertainment options in Johannesburg are as varied as the city itself. The "City of Gold" provides a wide range of alternatives to make sure your evenings are as amazing as your days, whether you're seeking to dance the night away, take in some live music, or just enjoy a peaceful evening with a beverage. Just keep in mind to explore properly and to enjoy this vibrant city's vibe!

Dos and don't in Johannesburg

It's important to be aware of certain dos and don'ts while visiting Johannesburg, the vivacious and culturally rich "City of Gold," to guarantee a safe, pleasurable, and courteous trip. Let's explore these recommendations so you can confidently travel around this vibrant South African metropolis.

What to do in Johannesburg:

1. Do value diversity: Johannesburg is a kaleidoscope of ethnicities, languages, and customs. Accept this variety and take advantage of the chance to discover the fascinating history and legacy of the city's many populations.

2. While there are many safe spots in Johannesburg, it's vital to be cautious, particularly in certain districts. Use trustworthy transportation providers, exercise caution, and refrain from exhibiting costly stuff.

3. Do Make an Effort to Acquire Some Local Phrases:** South Africans value tourists who make an effort to acquire a few fundamental phrases in one of the nation's 11 official languages, such as isiZulu, isiXhosa, or Sesotho.

4. Try South African Food: South African food is an exciting gastronomic experience. Try local specialties including "biltong" (cured pork that has been dried), "bunny chow," and "boerewors"

(sausage). From fast food to upscale dining, Johannesburg has a range of eating alternatives.

5. Respect wildlife: Follow the guidelines for wildlife watching and conservation if you want to visit any parks or reserves in the Johannesburg region.

6. Even though credit cards are often accepted, it's a good idea to have some cash on hand for smaller transactions and in case you go to places where card payments are less prevalent.

7. Do Dress Modestly: When visiting rural areas or places of religion, dress politely and modestly. In general, South Africans like when foreigners are sensitive to their culture.

What not to do in Johannesburg:

1. Avoid wearing expensive jewelry, carrying large sums of cash, or exhibiting costly objects: To reduce the chance of theft, stay away from costly objects like cameras or cellphones in busy or unfamiliar settings.

2. Don't Wander Alone at Night: It's better to see Johannesburg's entertainment and nightlife zones with friends or under the guidance of a dependable local guide. Remain in bright, crowded locations.

3. Don't Engage in Risky Behavior: Refrain from engaging in unlawful or drug-related activities. Drug offenses are subject to harsh punishments in South Africa.

4. Don't Forget Sun Protection: Because Johannesburg has a warm, sunny environment, it's important to apply sunscreen and take precautions against the sun's harmful rays, particularly in the summer.

5. Don't trek alone: It's not a good idea to trek alone, particularly in rural places, if you want to explore hiking routes or natural reserves. Tell someone about your intentions and when you anticipate returning.

6. Respect Local Customs: South Africa is home to a wide variety of cultures and customs. Be

aware of regional traditions and show respect for those that are unique to various groups.

7. Avoid drinking and driving: South Africa's legal blood alcohol level is relatively low. Use public transit, a designated driver, or ridesharing services instead of driving after drinking.

You may have a safe and fun time while seeing Johannesburg if you keep to these dos and don'ts. Remember to respect the traditions of the people you interact with, take reasonable safety measures, and enjoy the friendliness and hospitality that South Africa is renowned for. By exercising caution and respect when visiting Johannesburg, you may fully enjoy everything that this vibrant city has to offer in terms of history, culture, and natural beauty.

Chapter 3

Getting to know Johannesburg's history

The Journey through History at the Apartheid Museum

A significant and moving memorial to the tumultuous history of apartheid in South Africa is the Apartheid Museum in Johannesburg. It serves as a potent reminder of South Africa's people's hardships and victories in their pursuit of freedom, equality, and justice.

As soon as you enter the museum, apartheid's formal start in 1948 and end in the early 1990s are both quickly brought to mind. With two entrances, one for "whites" and one for "non-whites," the museum's design itself is significant and reflects the racial segregation prevalent at the time. The emotional journey that lies ahead is set in motion by this architectural decision.

The museum's interior has well-chosen displays that provide visitors with a thorough grasp of apartheid's historical context, the havoc it wreaked on South African society, and the valiant resistance it inspired. The museum tour takes you chronologically through the worst periods of apartheid's history.

History is brought to life via images, movies, testimony from actual people, and artifacts. The notorious "pass books" that restricted non-white residents' movements will be on display, and you'll discover how the Group Areas Act forcefully evicted individuals from their houses based on their race. The museum doesn't sugarcoat the atrocities of apartheid, making for a very poignant visit.

The Apartheid Museum's commitment to sharing the tales of both the oppressors and the oppressed is among its most remarkable qualities. It does more than just disparage one group or champion another. Instead, it gives the whole thing a human face by illuminating the complexity of apartheid and the people who participated in it in diverse ways.

The museum offers visitors the chance to interact with it personally. To imitate the unfairness and unpredictability of apartheid's racial classifications, you'll be given a randomly chosen racial classification upon admission, either "white" or "non-white." It's a simple yet powerful technique for assisting you in understanding the feelings of people who experienced this time period.

You will come across tales of perseverance and resistance along the way. The museum honors the valiant people who stood out for change, including Desmond Tutu and Nelson Mandela, as well as numerous other unsung heroes. Their tales arouse optimism and demonstrate the effectiveness of group effort.

The story of South Africa's early 1990s transition to democracy, which was highlighted by Nelson Mandela's release from jail and the country's first democratic elections, is the journey's climax at the Apartheid Museum. This transformation, which is sometimes referred to as a "miracle," is evidence of the South African people's unwavering spirit and dedication to rapprochement.

The Apartheid Museum is a live history lesson and a celebration of the tenacity of the human spirit; thus, it is more than simply a museum. It encourages visitors to think about the present, examine the past, and contribute to a future that is more inclusive and equitable. Anyone who wants to comprehend the complexity of apartheid and the continuing strength of optimism and solidarity should go there.

Exploring Soweto: The Center of Change

Soweto, which stands for "South Western Townships," is more than just a location on a map; it's a live, breathing example of the tenacity and spirit of a neighborhood that had a significant influence on South Africa's history. This large metropolitan region, immediately southwest of Johannesburg, is often referred to as the "Birthplace of Change" because of its significant contribution to the fight against apartheid and the change of South African society.

You enter a vast fabric of history, culture, and community when you enter Soweto. It is a location where narratives converge and the past, present, and future are intimately connected. It is a location where the fight for justice, equality, and human rights is embodied.

Vilakazi Street, a seemingly regular street with great historical importance, is one of Soweto's most recognizable sights. One could ponder why. Well, it's the only street in the whole world that can claim Nelson Mandela and Desmond Tutu as previous inhabitants. Visitors may enter the rooms where Mandela lived and thought about the road to liberation in his old house, which is now a museum. Standing where such important choices were made is a humbling experience.

The Hector Pieterson Memorial and Museum, named after a 12-year-old child cruelly slain by police during the 1976 Soweto Uprising, is also located in Soweto. Because it sparked indignation and attention on a global scale, this incident represented a turning point in the fight against apartheid. In addition to honoring Hector, the museum also pays tribute to the numerous other people who gave their lives in defense of freedom.

You'll come across lively marketplaces, humming townships, and a complex tapestry of ethnicities as you stroll the streets of Soweto. It is a location where modern urban life coexists in special harmony with traditional African cultures. Soweto residents are kind and open to tourists from over the globe, and they are ready to share their culture and customs with them.

Soweto is a vibrant, changing community with a bright future; it is not simply about the past. With advancements in infrastructure, education, and healthcare, the township has seen substantial growth in recent years. However, the problems of unemployment and poverty continue, serving as a constant reminder that we are still fighting for a better life.

Beyond its boundaries, Soweto's spirit of evolution and resiliency is evident. It represents hope for those living in difficult situations all across the globe. It serves as a reminder that when regular people band together in the pursuit of a shared objective, they can do incredible things.

In conclusion, Soweto is more than just a location; it is a real-life example of perseverance in the face of persecution, victory over hardship, and the human spirit. It's a location where change has left its mark on every street corner and where future generations continue to be inspired by it. Anyone interested in learning about South Africa's rich, beautiful, and revolutionary past should go to Soweto.

Constitution Hill: Observer of Change

Constitution Hill, a historic location in the middle of Johannesburg, South Africa, is also a monument to the tremendous changes that have taken place in that country. This famous hill has seen some of South Africa's worst moments in history as well as, more significantly, its remarkable march toward justice, democracy, and human rights.

The first thing that hits you as you get closer to Constitution Hill is its towering architecture, which is a fusion of the ancient and the modern. It serves as a metaphor for how tyranny gives way to liberation. The area, which had housed an infamous jail complex where several political dissidents were detained during the apartheid period, has been converted into a symbol of hope and peace.

The Old Fort, a former jail that recounts the traumatic narrative of the past, is one of Constitution Hill's most compelling and eerie features. The prison's chilly, wet chambers, where numerous people were wrongfully detained, serve as a frightening reminder of apartheid's savagery. It is possible to observe the graffiti that was left on the cell walls as a reminder of the fortitude and defiance of the people who endured suffering there.

Constitution Hill nonetheless stands as a symbol of the victory of the human spirit, despite its melancholy past. The nation's dedication to justice and equality is symbolized by the Constitutional Court of South Africa, which is situated atop the hill. Here, the post-apartheid constitution of South Africa was drafted, creating the framework for a democratic and diverse nation.

The Constitutional Court's building itself is significant. It includes aspects of the Old Fort, tying the past and present together and highlighting how crucial it is to remember the past in order to create a better future. The court's doors include the inscription "The People Shall Govern," which serves as a reminder of the residents' authority.

Another area of Constitution Hill, the Women's Gaol, honors the valiant women who battled against apartheid. As you browse this area of the website, the tales of adversity and tenacity come to life, giving you a taste of the tremendous contributions made by women to the liberation cause.

Visitors are forced to face the complexity of South Africa's past as they go up Constitution Hill, which is a poignant experience. It serves as a space for introspection, remembering, and peace. A thorough knowledge of the transition from tyranny to democracy is provided via the museum's exhibits, interactive displays, and guided tours.

Constitution Hill serves as a tangible example of how change is possible even in the face of apparently insurmountable obstacles. It serves as a space for acknowledging the past, celebrating the present, and looking forward. It acts as a ray of hope for all civilizations working toward justice and equality.

Conclusion: Constitution Hill is more than simply a historical landmark; it is a tangible illustration of the value of justice, the strength of human resilience, and the persevering spirit of a country. For anybody hoping to observe how South Africa's democracy has developed, it is a must-visit location. It serves as a symbol of transition and healing.

Chapter 4

Johannesburg's famous places and attractions

Maboneng Precinct: A Center for Art and Culture

Maboneng Precinct, in the center of Johannesburg, South Africa, is a compelling and energetic hub. It serves as evidence of the ability of urban renewal and the blending of art and culture to change a region. By lighting the city's environment with creativity, inventiveness, and a special feeling of community, Maboneng, a Sotho term that means "place of light," has certainly lived up to its name.

Maboneng stands out for its ability to adroitly combine the ancient and modern. Developers and artists who recognized the potential in this hitherto neglected area of the city worked with vision to bring it to life. The precinct's intriguing blend of modern buildings and repurposed warehouses creates a visually appealing setting that serves as a blank canvas for creative creation.

The lifeblood of Maboneng is art. The district is filled with galleries, workshops, and outdoor projects that display a wide variety of creative styles and materials. It is a location where traditional African art meets contemporary and experimental forms, weaving a vibrant tapestry that represents South Africa's rich cultural legacy and the current state of the international art scene.

Maboneng is a cultural mash-up that is more than simply about art. The precinct's streets are dotted with cafés, eateries, and shops that give visitors a sense of the many tastes and styles that define Johannesburg's metropolitan character. It's a spot where you can eat delectable food from all over the globe, drink creative cocktails, and have intriguing discussions with locals and other tourists.

Maboneng's population is as varied as its products. The precinct has drawn a diverse group of artists, businesspeople, and other creatives, producing an atmosphere that values cooperation and creativity. As you wander the region, you can feel this sense of community, and it's not unusual to start up a discussion with a local designer or artist who is ready to share their enthusiasm.

Maboneng comes alive all year with a program of activities that honor art, culture, and community. There is always something going on here, from markets and cinema screenings to live concerts and art exhibits. The neighborhood has emerged as a hub for Johannesburg's cultural scene, luring both residents and visitors looking for an immersive and real-world experience.

In conclusion, Maboneng Precinct is a fantastic example of how art and culture can revitalize urban areas. It's a place where creativity has no limitations, where the past and present live together, and where a sense of community is strong. Maboneng encourages you to explore, discover, and be inspired by the limitless manifestations of human ingenuity that light up this special "place of light" in Johannesburg, whether you're an art aficionado, a gourmet, or just someone wanting to soak up the colorful environment.

Green Oasis in the Johannesburg Botanical Garden

Often referred to as the city's "green oasis," Johannesburg Botanical Garden is a tranquil and charming retreat tucked away in the middle of South Africa's busy metropolis. Inviting visitors to immerse themselves in nature's calm while discovering a vast assortment of plant life, animals, and breathtaking scenery, this rich botanical jewel provides relief from the metropolitan clamor and bustle.

The Johannesburg Botanical Garden, which covers 81 hectares, is evidence of the city's dedication to protecting and honoring its natural heritage. Since its establishment in 1964, it has grown to be a beloved vacation spot for both residents and visitors, attracting nature lovers, families.

The garden's huge plant collection is one of its distinguishing qualities. It displays the astounding biodiversity of South Africa and the whole African continent, with more than 30,000 trees, shrubs, and blooming plants. You'll come across a stunning variety of colors, forms, and fragrances while strolling through the expertly designed gardens, from colorful native flowers to imposing foreign trees.

The garden provides a shelter for birds and other creatures in addition to being a sanctuary for flora. The garden is the ideal location for birding aficionados because of the wide variety of avian species that make it home, from sunbirds to weavers. The serene ponds and water features are home to a variety of aquatic species, which enhances the biological diversity of the garden.

The Johannesburg Botanical Garden has several relaxing areas for visitors wishing to unwind. Theme gardens, including the Shakespeare Garden, Rose Garden, and Herb Garden, are all nearby. You may set up a picnic under a large oak tree or stroll along the winding walkways. The background for a tranquil day is the sound of birds tweeting and leaves rustling in the wind.

With a special children's garden that provides an engaging and instructive experience, kids are well taken care of as well. Young explorers may gain a greater understanding of the natural world by participating in practical activities where they can learn about plants and ecosystems.

The garden serves as a center for environmental education and research as well as active enjoyment. It sponsors educational programs, excursions, and seminars that advance sustainability and conservation. This dedication to teaching highlights the garden's significance in promoting the value of protecting our planet's priceless ecosystems.

The Johannesburg Botanical Garden hosts a variety of activities all year long, including outdoor concerts, art exhibits, and plant sales. As a result of these events, the neighborhood becomes more cohesive and shares a love of the natural world.

The Johannesburg Botanical Garden is a tribute to the continuous relationship between urban life and the natural world and is more than simply a collection of plants, in my opinion. It serves as a timely reminder of the need to protect urban green areas, which provide a safe haven where people of all ages may get in touch with nature, learn about it, and find consolation. This lush haven in the middle of Johannesburg greets you with open arms, asking you to explore, discover, and relax in its timeless beauty. Whether you're an enthusiastic botanist, a nature lover, or just looking for a tranquil vacation, this green paradise welcomes you.

Sky-High Views from the Top of Africa

The stunning and unmatched experience provided by Top of Africa, positioned atop the Carlton Centre skyscraper in the center of Johannesburg, actually transports you to new heights. This observation deck, which is the highest structure in Africa, serves as a symbol of human creativity and offers tourists a genuinely breathtaking experience.

The Carlton Centre, which rises to a dizzying height of 223 meters (732 feet), is a work of architecture unto itself. The Top of Africa, which invites guests to climb to its top levels for a panoramic perspective of Johannesburg and its enormous metropolitan environment, is what really steals the show. You are treated to a 360-degree view from this vantage point that is unmatched in its ability to convey the spirit of the city.

The first leg of the ascent is a quick elevator ride that appears to defy gravity as it swiftly transports you above. You emerge onto the observation deck as the doors open to be welcomed with a stunning view. The famous Witwatersrand hills are seen in the background, framing the expansive city's expanse of skyscrapers, busy streets, and green areas.

The feeling of size that Top of Africa conveys is among its most impressive features. You get a new respect for Johannesburg's size from this vantage point. You may experience a deep feeling of connection to the urban fabric below as the city's numerous neighborhoods, varied populations, and rich history are exposed before your eyes.

The deck is built with both leisure and exploration in mind. There are relaxing spots where you can sit back and take in the scenery while soaking up the pulse of the city below. On a clear day, sights including the Nelson Mandela Bridge, the Johannesburg Art Gallery, and Ellis Park Stadium may be seen in the distance.

There is a chance for the more daring to take a snapshot of the occasion. Top of Africa is a great location for both amateur and professional photographers to capture the spirit of the city because of the constantly shifting interaction of light and shadow.

However, as day turns to night, Top of Africa really comes to life. The balcony becomes a beautiful and breathtaking location when the sun begins to set and Johannesburg's metropolis starts to glow with innumerable lights. This observation deck is a popular option for couples looking for a special date night because of the breathtaking transformation from the golden hour to a starry night sky.

The top of Africa is also a place for contemplation; it's not only about the view. It provides a brief respite from the bustle of the city, enabling you to consider the past, present, and future of the metropolis. It's a location where you can feel the energy of Johannesburg, a symbol of the city's tenacity and vitality.

To sum up, Top of Africa is more than simply an observation deck; it's a tour that, quite literally, enhances your viewpoint. It's a location where you can perch on the rim of the sky and take in the intricacy and beauty of a metropolis that has reached astounding heights.

Chapter 5

Johannesburg's Cultural Scene

<u>Markets for arts and crafts</u>

Johannesburg's arts and crafts markets provide a colorful and enthralling window into the city's diverse cultural fabric. These markets, which are dispersed across the city, provide a meeting place for tourists and a showcase for the varied creative traditions of South Africa.

The Rosebank Art and Craft Market is one of Johannesburg's most recognizable and lasting marketplaces. This market, which is located in the center of the affluent Rosebank district, has an appealing and unique charm. A kaleidoscope of hues, patterns, and textures will meet you as you browse the booths; each one represents a different aspect of South African tradition.

The handmade jewelry, beading, and traditional textiles seen at the Rosebank Art & Craft Market are famous. A great tribute to the artistry that has been handed down through the decades is the beautiful beading, which is often produced by talented Zulu artists. This market has an abundance of choices, whether you're searching for a colorful tapestry, a bejeweled bracelet, or a necklace made of beads.

The African Craft Market in Sandton's Nelson Mandela Square is a must-mention when discussing Johannesburg's art and craft marketplaces. This market honors the variety and craftsmanship of Africa. Everything from carvings and sculptures to fabrics and ceramics may be found here, representing the rich cultural legacy of the continent. Only a small sample of the creative delights awaiting tourists may be seen in the vibrant colors of Maasai blankets and the complex patterns of Shona stone sculptures.

Beyond the more well-known markets, Johannesburg also has a bustling street vendor and artisan culture that sets up shop in different districts, creating spontaneous marketplaces that teem with life and authenticity. Particularly in Maboneng Precinct, the urban environment of the city is transformed into a canvas for street art and a venue for outdoor markets. You can come across upcoming artists displaying their work here or discover one-of-a-kind handcrafted goods that are as varied as the residents of Johannesburg.

In addition to providing venues for artists and artisans to display their skills, art and craft fairs in Johannesburg also act as windows into the social and cultural dynamics of the city. They provide a setting where residents and visitors may interact with the legends and customs that have influenced South Africa's aesthetic character.

Additionally, by empowering craftspeople and encouraging sustainable livelihoods, these marketplaces have a tremendous positive impact on the local economy. You're not only getting a lovely souvenir when you buy an artwork or craft item at one of these markets; you're also helping the brilliant people whose work you're buying to sustain their careers.

In conclusion, Johannesburg's Arts and Crafts Markets are more than just places to buy; they're also fully immersing experiences that provide visitors with a close connection to the history, culture, and people of the city. These marketplaces entice with their vivid colors, rich textures, and the promise of learning more about South Africa's soul through the hands of its talented artists, whether you're an art aficionado, a collector, or just a curious tourist.

.

Festivals and music

In the fabric of human civilization, music and festivals are linked threads that combine rhythms, melodies, and emotions to produce experiences that are soul-stirring. These festive gatherings bring individuals from all origins together across boundaries and tongues, thanks to the unifying power of music.

Festivals, in all their manifestations, have played a significant role in human history for many years. Festivals have long been a means for communities to come together, express their identity, and find significance in common rituals, from ancient religious celebrations and harvest festivals to modern music and art gatherings. They demonstrate how important connection, expression, and celebration are to us.

The music festival is one of the most recognizable and lasting forms of festival. These multi-day events are sensory overloads of sound, color, and energy where performers and festival-goers alike join together to create an environment of unbridled joy. Music festivals provide a variety of experiences to suit any musical preference, whether it is the throbbing rhythms of electronic dance music at Tomorrowland, the rock 'n' roll energy of

Glastonbury, or the diverse blending of genres at Coachella.

Music festivals are about more than simply the main performers; they're also about the shared experience. It's the sensation of being a part of something greater than oneself when surrounded by a large crowd and bopping to the music. It's the bonding through shared laughs, the acquaintances who become friends, and the feeling of liberation that comes from dancing outside beneath the stars.

Festivals often provide venues for creative expression and cultural discovery in addition to music. They include interactive installations, performance art, and visual arts that appeal to the senses of festival guests. Visitors are urged to actively engage in the creative process as these events transform into live canvases where creativity has no limitations.

The role music festivals play in defining the identity of towns and regions is intriguing. Inseparable from the cultural character of their individual towns, iconic events like Austin's South by Southwest (SXSW) and New Orleans' Jazz Fest attract tens of thousands of tourists each year and contribute millions of dollars to the local economy. These occasions turn ordinary locations into thriving centers of creativity and innovation.

Additionally, music festivals have the ability to spark social and political revolutions. These gatherings have a special potential to elevate voices and spur change, from Woodstock's importance in the counterculture movement of the 1960s to more modern festivals supporting social and environmental concerns. They operate as forums for activists to inspire and motivate others as well as for artists to express their thoughts.

Music festivals now have a wider audience than ever before, thanks to the internet era. People from all around the globe may now interact and enjoy the festival experience thanks to online communities, live-streamed concerts, and virtual festivals. This has increased the accessibility of festivals by enabling individuals who may not have the wherewithal to physically attend to still experience some of the enchantment.

In conclusion, music and festivals are about more than simply having fun; they're also about honoring the human spirit, establishing relationships, and making lifelong memories. They are evidence of our common love of music as well as our need to socialize, dance, and be affected by sound. Music and festivals serve as a constant reminder of the beauty and unity that can be found in the world of art and culture, whether you're swaying to jazz musicians in a park, dancing in a muddy field, or watching a performance from the comfort of your home.

Theaters and Events in Johannesburg

The theaters and performances in Johannesburg provide a dynamic blend of many creative forms that appeal to both residents and tourists, providing a thrilling view into the city's cultural pulse. This busy town has a thriving cultural sector that is both a reflection of its nuanced past and a beacon of inventiveness, with everything from avant-garde theaters to classic playhouses.

The Market Theatre is among the most recognizable theaters in the city. The Market Theatre, located in the center of Johannesburg's Newtown cultural district, is famous for its dedication to creating audacious, thought-provoking performances that address urgent social and political concerns. The theater, which was founded during the apartheid period, was crucial in cultivating opposition and advancing change through the arts. It still serves as a platform for creativity and storytelling today, presenting ground-breaking plays, provocative dramas, and cutting-edge performances that defy expectations and spark conversation.

The Joburg Theatre in Braamfontein is a great treasure for anyone looking for a more conventional theatrical experience. With its elaborate architecture and opulent interiors, this enormous, historic venue is a tribute to the city's rich cultural past. It presents a wide range of shows, including Broadway-style musicals, classical dramas, and opera and ballet of the highest caliber. The Joburg Theatre is a place where the creative vitality of the present coexists harmoniously with the elegance of the past.

The POPArt Theatre is a shining example of independent and fringe theater in the thriving Maboneng area. Emerging playwrights, performers, and directors have a space to experiment with their art in this small setting, often breaking rules and defying traditions. POPArt's diverse schedule of performances, which ranges from cutting-edge dramas to immersive and interactive theatrical experiences, makes it a destination for individuals looking for original and unusual stories.

The theatrical culture in Johannesburg spreads out into public areas and unusual locations rather than being restricted to conventional playhouses. The city's parks and streets often come alive with street art festivals, pop-up theater, and spontaneous performances that highlight the unadulterated talent of local artists. These unplanned instances of creative expression may be found everywhere, surprising and astonishing anyone who comes upon them.

Johannesburg also celebrates its rich cultural diversity with a variety of festivals and events in addition to these well-known places. For instance, the National Arts Festival is a well-known event on the cultural calendar that draws musicians and artists from all over the world. Theater, music, dance, and visual arts come together in this creative mashup to create a vivacious celebration of African culture.

Additionally, Johannesburg's theaters and performances have been crucial in promoting social cohesiveness and discourse in addition to providing entertainment. Artists have used them as venues to discuss difficult topics like identity, inequality, and reconciliation. The arts have been a potent tool for healing, comprehension, and change in a city with a turbulent past like Johannesburg.

Finally, the theaters and shows in Johannesburg are evidence of the city's creative vigor and cultural resiliency. They represent the culture, ambitions, and inventive spirit of South African society and provide a window into its intricate fabric. For anybody willing to investigate, Johannesburg's rich and varied cultural scene offers a world of engaging experiences, whether you're looking for cutting-edge theater, classical performances, or unanticipated creative encounters.

Chapter 6

Outdoor Adventures in Johannesburg

Safaris in the Wild Near Johannesburg

Although South Africa's biggest city, Johannesburg, may not be the first destination that springs to mind when considering a wildlife safari, it is a great site to begin your exploration of some of the nation's most amazing natural beauties. Johannesburg is the perfect center for wildlife aficionados since it is close to several famous national parks and wildlife reserves.

The Pilanesberg Game Reserve, which is around two and a half hours' drive from Johannesburg, is one of the most well-known wildlife locations close to the city. Due to its position within the crater of a long-gone volcano, Pilanesberg is special because it has a diversified terrain that is home to the Big Five (lion, elephant, buffalo, leopard, and rhinoceros) as well as many other intriguing species. Game drives in Pilanesberg provide a fantastic opportunity to see these famous creatures in their natural environment.

The Madikwe Game Reserve is another fantastic choice if you want an even more comprehensive animal encounter. Madikwe provides a malaria-free environment and is home to an astonishing variety of animals, despite being somewhat further away—about a four- to five-hour journey from Johannesburg. The reserve is renowned for its conservation initiatives and for its success in reintroducing threatened species, such as the African wild dog.

The Lion & Safari Park, just a 45-minute drive from Johannesburg, provides a taste of the African bush for those looking for a short getaway from the city. Here, you may get up close and personal with a wide range of creatures, such as lions, cheetahs, and wild dogs. They also get the rare chance to engage with lion cubs that have been raised by humans.

The Dinokeng Game Reserve, which is about an hour's drive from Johannesburg, is another natural treasure in the area. Dinokeng is the first free-roaming Big Five residential game reserve in Gauteng and provides a variety of opportunities for wildlife viewing, birding, and even hot air balloon safaris for another viewpoint on the continent.

The ideal time to visit must be taken into account while organizing a wildlife safari. The climate in South Africa varies, and several seasons might provide unique opportunities to see animals. Animals congregate near water sources during the dry winter months (May to September), making it easier to see them. Contrarily, the wetter summer months (October to April) are excellent for birding and beautiful scenery, but they may make it more difficult to see animals.

It's essential to choose a reputable tour company or resort that places an emphasis on conservation and ethical tourism while going on a wildlife safari close to Johannesburg. Many lodges offer all-inclusive packages that include game drives, cozy lodgings, and knowledgeable guides who may provide insightful information about the local flora and animals.

As a result, Johannesburg serves as an excellent entry point for seeing South Africa's natural beauties in all their magnificence, whether you're an experienced wildlife lover or a novice safari traveler. You might find yourself surrounded by the untamed grandeur of the African bush, only a few hours' drive from the busy metropolis, making experiences that will last a lifetime.

Trails for hiking and nature

Without a doubt, let's explore Johannesburg's hiking and natural paths. Although Johannesburg is sometimes linked to its urban bustle, it's important to note that the city also provides a variety of picturesque trails and outdoor getaways that are ideal for hikers and wildlife lovers alike.

A hidden treasure, the Walter Sisulu National Botanical Garden is situated in the Roodepoort region. It's not only about the magnificent waterfall; there are also a number of pathways that meander through the luxuriant native vegetation. You may explore a variety of pathways, from shorter ones that are good for kids to longer, harder alternatives for experienced hikers. There is a good possibility of seeing Verreaux's eagles flying above and excellent birdwatching in this area.

Kloofendal Nature Reserve is a great option if you're looking for a peaceful hiking experience right in the middle of Johannesburg's West Rand. The area offers well-delineated hiking routes that meander through attractive settings, including grassy fields and rocky outcrops. Watch out for the local dassies (rock hyraxes), who often bask in the sun on the rocks.

Melville Koppies Nature Reserve: This city nature reserve provides a unique synthesis of heritage and unspoiled beauty. It is located in the eccentric suburb of Melville and has walking paths that snake through historic archaeological ruins, native greenery, and breathtaking metropolitan skyline vistas. It's a great location for a tranquil getaway from the urban jungle.

Suikerbosrand Nature Reserve is around an hour's drive from Johannesburg and definitely worth the journey if you're ready to go a little farther. With a vast network of paths that highlight the Highveld's different ecosystems, this reserve is a hiker and wildlife lover's dream. Zebras, antelope, and a vast range of bird species are among the animals you may anticipate seeing.

The Magaliesberg Mountains, which are just a short drive from Johannesburg, provide a variety of hiking possibilities for hikers of all skill levels. Here, trails take you through rocky terrain, old woods, and beside riverbanks. You may add a cultural component to your outdoor journey by stopping at charming local artisan stores and eateries while hiking in this region.

Although located in the adjacent city of Pretoria rather than Johannesburg, the Lion's Head Trail is nevertheless important to highlight. This famous summit provides a quick but strenuous walk that rewards hikers with magnificent views of the city. It's a well-liked location for treks at dawn and dusk, and the ascent is thrilling.

When trekking, keep in mind to exercise prudence by bringing water, donning the proper attire, and alerting someone about your intentions. It's a good idea to check ahead of time and, if required, reserve your place since many of these trails charge admission fees.

Johannesburg's hiking and nature path options give a welcome chance to reconnect with nature in a city that is often known for its urban expansion. Johannesburg and its surrounds have plenty to offer every hiker and lover of nature, whether you're looking for a leisurely walk in a botanical garden or a strenuous climb in the mountains.

Sport and water recreation

Without a doubt, let's investigate the exciting water sports and entertainment scene in Johannesburg. Even though the city is located in the Highveld, far from the coast, there are still plenty of water-related activities there. For individuals who like the water and want to cool down on a hot day, Johannesburg and its surroundings offer a surprising variety of alternatives.

Emmarentia Dam is a local favorite for picnics and water sports, and it is located right in the center of Johannesburg. Canoeing, rowing, and stand-up paddleboarding are all excellent on the dam. You may either bring your own boat or hire one on-site. It's the perfect place to relax after a long week, thanks to the serene and lush surroundings.

A big reservoir with a variety of water sports is located at Hartebeespoort Dam, which is about an hour's drive from Johannesburg. This dam offers a variety of water sports, including sailing, jet skiing, parasailing, and even hot air ballooning. Awe-inspiring views of the dam and the neighboring Magaliesberg Mountains may be seen from the adjacent Harties Cableway.

River rafting is a popular activity, and the Vaal River, which is close to Johannesburg, is a great place to do it. Everyone, from novice to expert rafters, may use the Vaal since it has a variety of rapids. It's a great way to spend a day outside and increase your heart rate.

Windsurfing and kitesurfing: The Vaal Dam is a major location for these sports. These thrilling water activities are well suited to its wide-open seas and steady breeze. If you're new to these hobbies, there are many schools and rental stores in the region that can get you started.

The Aquatic Center at Wahooz is a water paradise and can be found in the Boksburg neighborhood of Wahooz. It offers a selection of water sports, including wakeboarding, water skiing, and kneeboarding. For specialists wishing to sharpen their abilities or novices eager to learn, this area's cableway system is ideal.

You can go scuba diving in Johannesburg, that's for sure! Despite being far from the ocean, the city is home to a number of diving schools that provide instruction and excursions to neighboring quarries. A three-hour journey from Johannesburg, the Wondergat diving location is well-known for its pristine waters and underwater caverns, making it a favorite among divers.

Adventure Water Parks: Johannesburg boasts a few adventure water parks, including the Bambanani Water Park, if you're searching for family-friendly water fun. These parks provide pools, lazy rivers, and water slides, making them ideal for a day of family fun in the heat.

Always put safety first while participating in water activities. This entails donning life jackets, paying attention to local laws, and acting in accordance with instructors' or guides' directions. Check the seasons and operation times for these water-based activities as well, since they might change.

Therefore, although lacking the coastline of Cape Town or Durban, Johannesburg more than makes up for it with its variety of water sports and leisure activities. The city of Johannesburg has lots to offer thrill-seekers eager for high-speed experiences as well as those who just want to unwind by the river.

Chapter 7

Shopping in Johannesburg

<u>Shop in style at Sandton City Mall</u>

An elegant and opulent shopping location is Sandton City Mall. This renowned mall, which is located in the heart of Sandton in Johannesburg, South Africa, is a model of elegance and refinement for other shopping centers.

You'll notice the mall's striking exterior as you get closer; it gives away something about the splendor that awaits within. The architectural style, which combines contemporary with vintage appeal, creates a welcoming environment for customers from all walks of life.

You'll be welcomed by a world of upscale brands, boutiques, and designer shops as soon as you enter. A destination for individuals who value the finest things in life, Sandton City Mall is recognized for having a large selection of designer names. Every fashion choice and taste may be catered to here, from well-known worldwide brands to homegrown South African designers.

The inside of the mall is decorated with lovely art pieces and lush vegetation, creating a relaxing atmosphere while you browse the many stores and boutiques. The Sandton City Mall is your one-stop shop for the newest styles in clothing, fine jewelry, and cutting-edge technology.

The mall provides a lovely mix of cafés, restaurants, and eateries for when you need a break from shopping. Enjoy a fine dinner, a cup of freshly made coffee, or a sweet treat while soaking up the lively ambiance of this shopping haven.

The Sandton City Mall is more than simply a place to shop; it is a unique experience. The mall presents several events and exhibits all year, enhancing your stay with a touch of culture and enjoyment. There's always something going on to keep you interested and amused, whether it's a fashion show, an art exhibit, or a live concert.

You'll also notice the variety of consumers as you go around the mall, which is indicative of Sandton's international vibe. People from all walks of life go there to enjoy the art of shopping and the thrill of unearthing hidden gems.

The Sandton City Mall offers a variety of shop options in addition to practical features including plenty of parking, simple access, and helpful concierge services. It was created to meet the requirements of its customers, delivering a smooth and pleasurable purchasing experience.

In summary, Sandton City Mall is more than simply a mall; it's a lifestyle destination where you can eat elegantly, shop stylishly, and immerse yourself in a world of luxury and fashion. So, whether you're a fashion enthusiast or just looking for a fun day out, Sandton's famed mall is the place to be. Visit Sandton City Mall to see the pinnacle of retail excellence!

African traditional markets

A colorful and educational adventure may be started by visiting Johannesburg's traditional African marketplaces. These markets serve as more than simply shopping destinations; they are vibrant centers of African culture, creativity, and community.

The Rosebank Sunday Market is one of Johannesburg's most well-known traditional marketplaces. The rooftop of the Rosebank Mall is transformed into a buzzing tangle of colorful kiosks and animated conversation every Sunday. You'll find a wealth of African workmanship right here. This market displays an astounding range of African art, from hand-carved wooden sculptures that capture the spirit of the continent to beaded jewelry that recounts tales of local tribes.

The scent of authentic African food fills the air, luring you to tempting dishes like rabbit chow, boerewors rolls, and samoosas. Enjoy the delicious and varied cuisine of the continent, from fiery West African food to South African delights.

You'll be serenaded by the rhythmic sounds of live drumming performances as you stroll around the market; they inject the space with a contagious vibrancy. The market often hosts talented street musicians and entertainers who provide a thrilling soundtrack to your shopping experience.

The neighborhood goods market in the thriving area of Braamfontein is another well-known market in Johannesburg. The items that are made and obtained locally are celebrated at this market. A variety of artisanal products, including organic food and handcrafted clothing and design items, are available here. You may speak with the artists who made the goods there, and South African inventiveness is on display there.

The Mai Mai Market is a hidden treasure for anyone who is interested in traditional African clothing. This market is a maze of booths offering traditional costumes, beads, and textiles that are tucked away in the center of the city. It's a chance to delve into the diverse array of African clothing, where each item narrates a particular tale about culture and tradition.

The feeling of community that these marketplaces generate is what makes them unique. You'll get the opportunity to interact with local sellers, find out more about their wares, and maybe even see them make their works of art in front of your own eyes. It offers an opportunity to interact with the people and customs that make Johannesburg a mash-up of African cultures.

It's not just about buying when you explore Johannesburg's traditional African marketplaces;

it's about getting to know Africa. You may leave with more than just trinkets from these markets; you can also get a greater understanding of the rich tapestry of African life and culture. These marketplaces provide a window into the dynamic, diverse character of the continent. Therefore, if you ever find yourself in Johannesburg, make a point of exploring these markets for a once-in-a-lifetime experience that will leave you with priceless mementos and souvenirs from the heart of Africa.

Old and Strange Findings

For those looking for vintage and one-of-a-kind discoveries, Johannesburg, a city renowned for its rich history and cultural variety, is a treasure trove. Johannesburg has a wide range of options to discover hidden treasures and connect with the past, from antique trinkets to one-of-a-kind works of art.

The Nelson Mandela Square Antique Fair is among the best sites to begin your search for old treasures. This market, which takes place on certain weekends, is a sanctuary for fans of antiques. You may peruse the booths here, which are packed with antique furniture, retro décor, and timeless items. Each object offers a fascinating window into South Africa's past, as if it were whispering tales of days gone by.

The African Craft Market in Rosebank is a must-visit location for anyone with an interest in African arts and crafts. This crowded market offers a wide variety of homemade goods, from stunning wooden masks to elaborate beading. It's a chance to buy distinctive mementos while simultaneously promoting regional artists and their time-honored skills.

A flourishing network of art studios and galleries can be found in Johannesburg, where you may find modern artwork that is both distinctive and captivating. In particular, the Maboneng Precinct stands out as a center for artistic expression. Visit galleries like the David Krut Projects to view pieces by known and up-and-coming artists that push the limits of modern art.

44 Stanley is a hip location that satisfies your cravings for retro clothing if you're looking for vintage attire. This former industrial complex is now home to a variety of boutiques and stores that provide carefully chosen vintage apparel, accessories, and home furnishings. You may locate the ideal statement item there to up your sense of style.

The Collectors Treasury in the center of Johannesburg is a bookworm's paradise. This multi-story bookshop is a maze of shelves filled with out-of-print, rare, and antique books, old atlases, and vintage periodicals. It offers a chance to travel through time by reading old books; thus, it's more than simply a location to buy books.

The feeling of adventure offered by looking for vintage and one-of-a-kind items in Johannesburg is what makes it distinctive. Whether it's an old record with the crackles of history in its grooves or an old piece of furniture that has seen decades of change, every object you find has a tale to tell. You may connect with the city's rich legacy via this trip through time, culture, and innovation.

In conclusion, Johannesburg's selection of vintage and one-of-a-kind items is a monument to the city's rich cultural heritage and active past. Johannesburg's markets, galleries, and boutiques provide a fascinating tapestry of the past and present that is just begging to be explored, whether you're an experienced collector or just an enthusiast seeking something unique. So start your adventure of exploration, and who knows, you could find a piece of history that speaks to your spirit and gives your life a bit of Johannesburg's own charm.

Chapter 8

Johannesburg's Accommodation Options

Upscale inns and resorts

My able friend, I would be delighted to give you a thorough rundown of the upscale accommodations available in Johannesburg. The biggest city in South Africa is Johannesburg, sometimes known as Jozi or Joburg, and it is a thriving center for business, culture, and tourism. As a result, it has a wide selection of magnificent luxury hotels and resorts that appeal to discriminating tourists looking for the pinnacle of extravagance and comfort.

The Saxon Hotel, Villas, and Spa is one of Johannesburg's most recognizable opulent hotels. This magnificent sanctuary gives visitors a wonderful fusion of African warmth and modern luxury while nestled in the peaceful neighborhood of Sandhurst. The Saxon has opulent suites and villas that are exquisitely decorated and equipped with every conceivable contemporary convenience. In the middle of the city's bustle, the hotel's verdant gardens, koi ponds, and world-class spa provide a tranquil haven.

The Four Seasons Hotel Westcliff is another crowning achievement in Johannesburg's hotel industry. This opulent hotel, perched on a hillside, offers visitors stunning panoramic views of the city's lush green suburbs and the Johannesburg Zoo. The Four Seasons is famous for its flawless service, opulent accommodations, and mouth watering dining choices. The tranquil spa facilities and infinity pool provide the ideal escape from Johannesburg's bustling city life.

The Fairlawns Boutique Hotel and Spa is a hidden treasure for anyone looking for a more in-depth encounter with nature. This opulent hotel in Johannesburg is surrounded by eight acres of beautifully planted grounds and offers rooms with distinctive themes and a top-notch spa that caters to relaxation and regeneration. Amuse-Bouche, the on-site restaurant, is a gourmet treat that embraces both foreign and South African delicacies.

Johannesburg also has opulent resorts that provide a total retreat from the bustle of the city. Near O.R. lies the opulent D'Oreale Grande Hotel at Emperors Palace, a five-star haven. International Tambo Airport It has lavish accommodations, a casino, and a choice of eateries to tempt your palate.

The Maslow Hotel must be included while talking about opulent lodging in Johannesburg. The Maslow, which is located in the center of the Sandton business sector, is the pinnacle of contemporary luxury with its roomy accommodations, cutting-edge meeting spaces, and luxurious spa. Both business and leisure tourists will find it to be a refuge.

In addition to offering an opulent place to stay, Johannesburg's luxury hotels and resorts serve as entryways to the city's unique culture, history, and attractions. These places make sure that your trip to the City of Gold, whether you're there for business or pleasure, is nothing short of extraordinary.

Finally, despite the lively energy of this dynamic city, Johannesburg's luxury hotels and resorts provide a world of pleasure and refinement. These accommodations provide the ideal fusion of comfort, convenience, and elegance to make your stay genuinely extraordinary, whether you're looking for a peaceful getaway, a base for business operations, or an exploration of South Africa's cultural resources. Therefore, the city's amazing selection of luxury hotels and resorts is where you may stay if you're considering a trip to Johannesburg and want to experience the height of luxury hospitality.

Coziness of bed and breakfas

Let's delve into Johannesburg's beautiful bed and breakfast scene. These charming and tiny lodgings provide a lovely contrast in a city noted for its busy streets and dynamic urban energy, giving visitors a warm and customized experience that seems like a home away from home.

The Melville Turret Guesthouse is one of Johannesburg's most notable bed and breakfasts. This quaint business, located in the artistic community of Melville, emits a warm aura. The pleasant interior, verdant garden, and Victorian-style building transport visitors to a bygone age. Melville Turret guarantees an intimate and customized stay because of its small number of rooms, and hosts often know visitors by name. This B&B is the ideal getaway for anyone looking for a peaceful oasis close to the city's attractions.

Think about staying at the Munro Boutique Hotel for a sense of history and nostalgia. This bed and breakfast, located in a gorgeously renovated historic home, highlights Johannesburg's rich past while still offering contemporary conveniences. There are just a few rooms available at The Munro, and each is individually designed with a mix of antique and modern furniture. The gorgeous garden, patio outside, and delicious breakfasts all contribute to the allure of this hidden treasure.

The Parkwood Boutique Hotel and Guest House can be found in Parkhurst, a neighborhood known for its greenery. This bed and breakfast skillfully blends modern architecture with cozy amenities. The public spaces are decorated with regional artwork, and each room is carefully decorated to provide a feeling of location and culture. It's the ideal place to relax since the beautiful garden and outdoor pool area provide a peaceful retreat from the bustle of the city.

The Winston Hotel in the upscale neighborhood of Rosebank is another noteworthy choice.

Although The Winston is bigger than other conventional bed and breakfasts, it nonetheless has a cozy, welcoming feel. The Milner, the hotel's on-site restaurant, offers delectable cuisine, while the suites are attractively furnished with opulent facilities. The Winston achieves a compromise between the opulence of a boutique hotel and the attentive service of a B&B.

The friendly and attentive care offered by hosts, who often go above and beyond to ensure visitors have a pleasant stay, is what distinguishes these lodgings, in addition to the distinctive characteristics of each bed and breakfast. Staying at a welcoming bed and breakfast in the city gives you the ability to interact with residents and other tourists equally, offering individual breakfasts and insider information on discovering Johannesburg's hidden jewels.

In conclusion, inviting bed and breakfasts in Johannesburg provide a lovely substitute for conventional hotels by enabling visitors to fully experience the culture and history of the city while taking pleasure in a home-like atmosphere. These quaint places guarantee a friendly and wonderful experience in the center of South Africa's biggest city, whether you're looking for a romantic getaway, a serene retreat, or a chance to mingle with the locals. Therefore, if you're considering a trip to Johannesburg and want the cozy charm of a bed and breakfast, you may choose from a number of warm accommodations that will satisfy your needs for comfort, elegance, and hospitality.

Cost-effective Hostels

Thanks to the variety of inexpensive hostels that cater to tourists looking for reasonable but pleasant lodgings, seeing the dynamic and varied city of Johannesburg on a budget is not only feasible but also highly gratifying. These hostels are more than simply a place to sleep; they often operate as gathering places for people to mingle, share cultures, and create lifetime memories.

Curiocity Backpackers is one of Johannesburg's most well-liked cheap hostels. This hostel, which is located in the Maboneng Precinct of the city, offers guests more than simply a place to sleep; it also offers an unforgettable experience. The hostel has a lively environment with colorful paintings gracing its walls, a rooftop bar with spectacular city views, and a variety of lodging choices, including private rooms and dorms. It is common for tourists to meet with like-minded people and enjoy the city together when Curiocity organizes activities like city tours, art walks, and live music evenings.

Once in Joburg, a superb alternative situated in the vibrant Braamfontein district is still another great choice. This hostel offers both private rooms and dorm-style accommodations, combining price with a sense of community. The common facilities, which include a rooftop bar and lounge, are ideal for socializing with other guests. As a starting point for visiting surrounding sights like Constitution Hill and the neighborhood goods market, Joburg's central position is advantageous.

Lebo's Soweto Backpackers is a hidden treasure for tourists looking for a more laid-back setting. This hostel provides a special chance to learn about the history and culture of the neighborhood where it is located—the historic township of Soweto. Lebo, the hostel's proprietor, is renowned for his kind hospitality and provides escorted cycling and walking tours throughout Soweto, enabling visitors to learn more about the rich history of the township. There are possibilities for varied budgets, from shared dorms to private rondavels (traditional huts).

The Backpacker's Ritz, a warm and cost-effective option, can be found in the Kensington area. The hostel offers cozy shared and private accommodation choices, and its helpful staff is always there to provide advice on where to go. The common spaces, which include a pool and BBQ pits, invite visitors to mingle and unwind.

These inexpensive hostels in Johannesburg provide a genuine and worthwhile travel experience in addition to cost savings. They bring together tourists from all backgrounds, fostering a vibrant and varied environment where relationships are formed, tales are exchanged, and experiences are undertaken. Numerous of these hostels place a high priority on environmental operations, responsible tourism, and giving back to the neighborhood.

In conclusion, inexpensive hostels in Johannesburg provide visitors with a fantastic chance to see this exciting city without breaking the bank. They provide not only inexpensive lodging but also an opportunity to interact with other tourists, discover the local culture, and create lifelong experiences. These hostels in Johannesburg are prepared to welcome you with open arms and a feeling of adventure, whether you're a lone traveler looking for adventure, a backpacker on a limited budget, or just wanting a more communal and immersive travel experience. Pack your bags, reserve your lodging, and get ready to see everything that Johannesburg has to offer without sacrificing comfort or your budget.

Chapter 9

Transportation in the City

The city of Johannesburg's transportation system is a complex and evolving component of urban life. The biggest city in South Africa and a significant economic and cultural center on the African continent, this huge metropolis is situated in the Gauteng region. As a result, the city of Johannesburg's transportation system is crucial to both the growth of the city as a whole and the everyday lives of its citizens.

The road system in Johannesburg is among the most noticeable and crucial elements of the city's transportation system. The city is proud of its robust road system, which consists of a network of motorways, arterial roads, and local streets. As the intersection of the N1, N3, and N12 freeways, Johannesburg serves as a key regional transportation hub. This complex network of roadways links the city to other significant South African cities while facilitating the flow of people and products inside the city.

The city's road infrastructure, however, has several difficulties. For many commuters in Johannesburg, traffic congestion is a regular occurrence, prolonging travel times and raising irritation. The capacity of the city's road network has been stressed by both the city's fast population expansion and a rise in the number of cars on the road. Road enlargement initiatives, enhanced traffic control methods, and the creation of designated bus lanes have all been used to reduce congestion.

Another essential component of Johannesburg's urban mobility is public transit. A mix of buses, railroads, and minibus taxis make up the city's public transportation system. The Gautrain links Johannesburg with Pretoria and the O.R. with an advanced and effective commuter rail system. Tambo International Airport offers travelers a practical choice for getting to and from the city.

Despite playing a crucial role in the transportation scene, the minibus taxi sector has encountered issues with safety, regulation, and competition from other forms of public transportation. In order to raise safety standards and provide commuters with more dependable service, efforts have been undertaken to organize and regulate this industry.

Cycling and walking have become popular alternate modes of transportation in Johannesburg recently. Efforts to establish designated bike lanes and pedestrian-friendly areas are made to ease traffic, enhance air quality, and encourage citizens to lead healthier lifestyles.

Additionally, the introduction of ride-sharing services and the incorporation of smartphone transportation applications have changed how individuals move about the city. With their accessible and adaptable transportation alternatives, businesses like Uber and Bolt have become more popular.

The transportation environment in Johannesburg is not without its difficulties. The differences between prosperous, well-connected locations and neglected, underserved populations with no access to safe transportation show how unequal society is. Additionally, the city must address important problems, including safety, air pollution, and environmental sustainability.

In conclusion, the city of Johannesburg's transportation system is intricate and dynamic, reflecting the expansion and development of the metropolis. Continuous efforts to enhance and extend the transportation network seek to produce a more accessible and sustainable urban environment for all citizens, despite issues linked to congestion, safety, and equality. Johannesburg's transportation infrastructure will be essential in determining how lively and international the city will become as it develops further.

Traveling in Johannesburg

Getting around Johannesburg, the biggest and most populated city in South Africa, is an interesting adventure through a varied metropolitan environment. The city provides a range of transportation alternatives to meet your requirements, whether you're a resident making your way to work or a tourist taking in the sights.

Private cars are often used as the main form of transportation in Johannesburg. The large road system of the city is made up of a labyrinth of motorways, important thoroughfares, and neighborhood streets. In Johannesburg, the N1, N3, and N12 motorways converge, creating a vital transportation hub for the whole Gauteng region. Private vehicles provide flexibility and convenience, but they also add to the city's well-known traffic congestion, especially during rush hours.

In terms of mobility, public transit is essential in Johannesburg. The modern commuter rail system, the Gautrain, links the city to Pretoria and O.R. International Tambo Airport. Both regular commuters and tourists like this quick and dependable service since it provides an easy method to get around traffic and reach important locations.

A large part of public transit in Johannesburg is the ubiquitous and often brightly colored minibus taxis. These shared taxis provide a convenient and economical way to get around, but they may be congested and have a reputation for having unpredictable driving styles. In an effort to improve safety and service standards, this sector has been formalized and regulated.

The city's bus system, which is run by Metrobus, is an additional mode of public transportation. Metro Buses provide a more affordable and pleasant alternative to minibus taxis in several areas of Johannesburg. Rea Vaya, the city's BRT system, furthermore provides dedicated bus lanes, making it a dependable and effective method of transportation, particularly during rush hours.

Johannesburg has made progress in encouraging cycling and walking for people who want a more environmentally responsible and health-conscious method of exploring the city. In certain places, dedicated bike lanes have been built, providing bikers with safer paths. Urban renovation initiatives have also resulted in the development of pedestrian-friendly areas where people can wander, buy, and take in the city's bustling street life.

In Johannesburg, ride-sharing services like Uber and Bolt have become very popular. These mobile applications let users hail rides from local drivers, providing convenience and often affordable rates. The way people travel around the city has been changed by this technology-driven approach to transportation, making it simpler than ever to get where you're going.

It's crucial to recognize, meanwhile, that Johannesburg's transportation system also reflects social inequalities. Depending on where you reside in the city, you may or may not have easy access to dependable and efficient transit. Richer towns often have stronger connections, but underprivileged areas struggle because of their restricted access to public transportation.

As a result of the city's rich culture and quick development, moving around Johannesburg is a dynamic and ever-changing experience. There are several ways to get around this bustling metropolitan area, including personal vehicles, public transit, cycling, walking, and ride-sharing. The city of Johannesburg works to offer accessible and sustainable mobility solutions for all of its citizens and tourists as it continues to grow and handle its transportation issues.

Using public transit

Public transit is an essential part of everyday life in Johannesburg, sometimes known as "Jo'burg" by locals, a busy South African city. The efficient and sustainable movement of its inhabitants depends on a multitude of public transportation choices in this huge metropolis, which is renowned for its economic strength and cultural richness.

The Gautrain is a mainstay of Johannesburg's public transit network. The way locals and tourists move throughout the city and beyond has been changed by this contemporary commuter train network. Johannesburg, Pretoria, and the O.R. are all connected by it. Tambo International Airport serves as a crucial transit connection for the province of Gauteng. The Gautrain is a popular option for those who want to escape the severe traffic jams on the city's roadways since it provides speed, dependability, and comfort.

Another essential component of Johannesburg's public transit system is minibus taxis. These unusual cars, which are often decorated with artwork and catchphrases and are painted in vibrant hues, are a common sight on the city's roadways. Numerous individuals who depend on them for their everyday commutes consider minibus taxis to be lifelines. They run along a variety of routes. However, because of their sloppy driving practices and informal character, attempts are being made to regulate and professionalize this industry.

Johannesburg residents have yet another choice for public transportation thanks to Metrobus, a city-run bus service. Wide-ranging metrobus lines serve both core and peripheral districts. These buses are a popular option for many commuters since they provide a more uniform and pleasant alternative to minibus taxis.

In Johannesburg's attempts to enhance public transportation, the Rea Vaya bus rapid transit (BRT) system marks a crucial turning point. Rea Vaya provides a quicker and more dependable method to navigate throughout the city with dedicated bus lanes and contemporary stops. It cuts travel times and eases traffic congestion by connecting important places, including the University of Johannesburg, Soweto, and the central business district.

Johannesburg cyclists had cause for celebration as well. The city is doing its best to promote cycling as a practical form of transportation. To promote eco-friendly and healthy commuting choices, dedicated bicycle lanes and bike-sharing programs have been implemented. These programs foster a greener, more sustainable urban environment while simultaneously easing traffic congestion.

Another crucial component of public transit in Johannesburg is walking. Urban renovation initiatives undertaken by the city have resulted in the development of pedestrian-friendly areas, notably in the central business district. These locations promote urban walking, generating a thriving street life and a sense of neighborhood.

Notably, the introduction of ride-sharing services like Uber and Bolt has increased the comfort and adaptability of public transit in Johannesburg. These mobile applications provide locals and tourists with a substitute for conventional taxis and public transportation by enabling them to request trips from nearby drivers.

However, Johannesburg confronts transportation issues, much like many other big cities. Traffic jams continue to be a problem, and it is clear that wealthy districts and underprivileged populations have different transit options. The city's authorities continue to place a high premium on addressing these inequalities and providing all inhabitants with equitable, safe, and effective public transit.

In conclusion, Johannesburg's public transportation system is a dynamic and developing one that represents the expansion and variety of the city. Johannesburg has a wide variety of alternatives for getting around, from the contemporary efficiency of the Gautrain to the colorful minibus taxis, from the practicality of ride-sharing applications to the eco-friendly appeal of cycling and walking. The city strives to provide a more accessible and sustainable urban environment that meets the requirements of all its citizens as it continues to expand and invest in its transportation infrastructure.

Tips for Driving and Car Rentals

If you're on a road trip or visiting a new city, car rentals and driving advice might be important elements of your journey. In this article, we'll explore the world of vehicle rentals and provide some insightful driving advice to make sure your trip is worry-free, pleasurable, and safe.

Vehicle rentals:

Most places have easy access to car rental services, giving visitors the opportunity to explore at their own speed. When hiring a vehicle, keep the following in mind:

1. When possible, reserve your rental vehicle in advance, particularly during periods of high travel demand. This may assist you in securing the kind of car you need and sometimes even help you obtain a better rate.

2. Pick the Right Automobile: Decide on an automobile that best meets your requirements. Choose a bigger car with room for people and baggage if you are going with a family or a

group. A tiny automobile could be more practical and simpler to handle in congested locations for singles or couples traveling alone.

3. Insurance: Always take rental automobile insurance into account. Although your own vehicle insurance policy could provide some coverage, it's best to get extra insurance from the rental agency to minimize unforeseen charges in the event of accidents or damage.

4. Check the automobile: Before leaving, give the rental automobile a full inspection to look for any damage or problems. In order to prevent disagreements when you return the car, take pictures or videos of any dings or blemishes.

Driving advice:

Following your successful rental vehicle booking, remember these vital driving tips:

1. Learn About Local Rules: Traffic rules differ across different nations and areas. Spend some time learning about and becoming familiar with the local driving laws. Pay close attention to

traffic signs, speed restrictions, and regional traditions.

2. Drive on the Right Side of the Road: You must drive on the right side of the road in many nations. Make sure to adapt to the driving style in your area.

3. Use a GPS gadget or navigational software to help you find your route, particularly in strange places. This may lessen the anxiety caused by navigating unfamiliar roadways.

4. Remain Vigilant: Fatigue may play a big part in car accidents. Before beginning a lengthy trip, get adequate rest and stop often to keep your mind sharp.

5. Avoid distractions: Driving while distracted is a major contributor to accidents. Steer clear of distractions like using your phone or other devices while driving. If you need to make a call or look up instructions, stop.

6. Parking: Be aware of any limits or rules in effect locally. Unnecessary inconveniences

might result from towing or fines for illegally parked cars.

7. Be Wary of Your Speed: Adhere to posted speed restrictions and modify your speed as necessary to account for changing traffic, weather, and visibility on the road.

8. Driving Defensively: Always drive defensively, assuming other drivers' intentions and being ready to respond appropriately.

9. Follow local etiquette: local driving conventions in certain areas could be different from your norm. For instance, it can be expected for drivers to give way to pedestrians or allow others to join in traffic.

10. Carry a basic emergency kit in your rental vehicle, which should include a first aid kit, a flashlight, jumper cables, and any other items you may need.

You may improve your trip experience and make sure that you drive safely and comfortably on new roads by paying attention to this driving advice and suggestions for renting a vehicle. Keep in mind that every location has its own distinct driving obstacles and charms, so being prepared and flexible are essential for a successful drive.

Chapter 10

Going beyond Johannesburg

Johannesburg day trips

The dynamic South African metropolis of Johannesburg has a number of neighboring attractions that appeal to a range of interests, making planning day excursions from there an intriguing task. There are several locations within a comfortable driving distance of Johannesburg that are worth seeing, whether you're a nature lover, a history nerd, or just seeking a change of scenery.

A trip to the Cradle of Humanity is essential for anybody who values the beauty of the natural world. Only a short drive from Johannesburg, this UNESCO World Heritage Site is home to a wealth of fossil discoveries that provide insight into the progenitors of modern humans. One of the highlights is the Sterkfontein Caves, which provide guided excursions that take you deep down to explore these old tunnels.

The Lion and Safari Park is a terrific choice if you want to get up close and personal with some animals. This park, which is around 45 minutes from Johannesburg, enables guests to get up close and personal with a variety of animals, including lions, cheetahs, and giraffes. It's an exciting experience that's great for both families and animal lovers.

Soweto is an interesting place for a day trip that combines history and culture. This township, which is close to Johannesburg, was important in the fight against apartheid. You may go on guided tours that explore the region's rich history, see famous sites like the Hector Pieterson Museum, and even eat at neighborhood restaurants to experience authentic South African cuisine.

The Walter Sisulu National Botanical Garden is a quiet sanctuary just 30 minutes from Johannesburg if you're looking for a more sedate getaway. It's the ideal location for a leisurely walk among thick flora, and the addition of a flowing waterfall makes it even more appealing.

And last, the Nirox Sculpture Park is a hidden treasure for art enthusiasts. A beautiful collection of modern sculptures is shown there, which is an hour away from Johannesburg. The setting is gorgeous. It's a distinctive fusion of nature and art that may lead to a delightfully tranquil day out.

In conclusion, Johannesburg provides a wide range of day-trip choices to suit various tastes and interests. There are day trips waiting for you just beyond the busy city boundaries, whether you're interested in history or wildlife or just want to unwind in a stunning environment. Pack your luggage, hit the road, and leave Johannesburg for an unforgettable trip!

Traveling across South Africa

A compelling trip across a nation with an incredible mix of landscapes, cultures, and experiences is what exploring South Africa is like. Every tourist may find something to enjoy in South Africa, from the lively metropolitan centers to the untamed countryside.

The well-known city of Cape Town is one of the first places that often springs to mind when thinking about traveling in South Africa. Cape Town is a destination for people seeking a harmonic synthesis of natural beauty and urban refinement, nestled between the imposing Table Mountain and the glittering seas of the Atlantic Ocean. You may explore the historic Robben Island, ride a cable car to the top of Table Mountain for panoramic views, or just stroll around Bo-Kaap's vibrant streets.

The Garden Route extends out invitingly as it travels along the shore. You pass through verdant woods, unspoiled beaches, and attractive coastal communities like Knysna and Plettenberg Bay on this gorgeous trip. Tsitsikamma National Park's imposing cliffs provide heart-pounding activities like bungee jumping from Bloukrans Bridge.

For those who go inside, the Drakensberg Mountains provide a peaceful haven for hikers and wildlife lovers. Trekking, horseback riding, and birding are just a few of the outdoor pursuits made possible by the stunning peaks, undulating hills, and clear streams. The Drakensberg is also home to an abundance of San rock art, which provides a window into the area's prehistoric past.

South Africa is home to some of the most well-known safari locations in the world for wildlife aficionados. The "Big Five" (lion, elephant, buffalo, leopard, and rhinoceros) and numerous more species may be found in abundance at Kruger National Park, one of the biggest wildlife reserves on the continent. Game drives are nothing short of breathtaking as they wind through the park's many different habitats.

Without taking part in the country's rich cultural legacy, a trip to South Africa would fall short. The biggest city in the nation, Johannesburg, is a crossroads of eras and civilizations. You may wander around Maboneng Precinct, an urban arts and cultural center, or tour the Apartheid Museum to learn more about the nation's complicated history.

The ancient city of Durban is located in the province of KwaZulu-Natal, farther east. It is a region famous for its breathtaking beaches and lively Indian culture, where you can enjoy delectable curries and discover a unique fusion of customs.

There are many things to do in South Africa, from the untamed Karoo to the gorgeous winelands of Stellenbosch and Franschhoek. This nation is a treasure trove of experiences waiting to be found, whether you're drinking world-class wines, awestruck by ancient rock formations, or just taking in the warmth of South African hospitality.

An excursion that provides a wonderful mix of landscapes, cultures, and experiences is traveling across South Africa. It's a location where you can take in the unadulterated beauty of nature, explore intricate history, and make lifelong memories. Pack your luggage, set off on this amazing voyage, and let South Africa's beauty enchant you.

Organizing Your next trip

Planning your next trip to Johannesburg is thrilling because it has the promise of a lively culture, stunning scenery, and life-changing events. To guarantee a smooth and comfortable voyage, it's crucial to keep a few important factors in mind as you set off on your excursion. Let's get into the specifics of organizing your trip to this fascinating city in South Africa.

1. Determine Your Goal: Prior to everything else, decide why you're visiting Johannesburg. Are you interested in learning more about the

city's extensive history? Maybe you're an animal lover eager to visit the surrounding game reserves. Your timetable will take on more form once your objective is clear.

2. Create a budget: Set a reasonable spending limit for your vacation. Take into account costs for travel, lodging, meals, entertainment, and mementos. Your decisions will be guided by your budget, which will also help you avoid going beyond it.

3. Select the Appropriate Time to Visit: Even though Johannesburg has a moderate climate, the seasons might change. Based on your tastes, do some research on the ideal time to go. Warm weather is best experienced from November to February, while June to August bring lovely days and chilly evenings.

4. Travel documents that are secure: Make sure your passport is current, and research the visa requirements for your country of citizenship. Make sure you secure the relevant permits if

necessary, since South Africa has special entrance requirements.

5. Plan Your Route: Make a basic itinerary that incorporates the sights and experiences you want to have. The Apartheid Museum, Gold Reef City, and Lion Park are just a few of Johannesburg's many cultural, historical, and natural attractions. Give yourself enough time to explore the city and go on day excursions to adjacent places.

6. Accommodation: Choose lodgings that fit your interests and financial situation. Luxury hotels, inexpensive hostels, and welcoming guest houses are all available in Johannesburg. To choose the ideal accommodation, investigate reviews and locations.

7. Transportation: Determine how you will get to know Johannesburg. The city's public transportation network is well-developed and includes buses and the Gautrain, which links to the airport. If you want more freedom, think

about hiring a vehicle, particularly if you want to explore the region.

8. Safety precautions include: Despite the fact that Johannesburg's safety has increased over the years, caution is still advised. Keep your possessions secure, don't flaunt your things, and keep up with the most recent safety advice.

9. Medical Preparations: Before flying to South Africa, check with your healthcare professional about any required immunizations or health precautions. Make sure you have enough travel insurance to pay for unforeseen medical costs.

10. Pack sensibly: Bring the right clothes and accessories for the weather and the activities you want to do. A universal power adaptor, sunscreen, and bug repellent are important items to remember.

11. Adopt the regional culture: By sampling regional cuisine, conversing with residents, and studying the history of the city, you may fully experience Johannesburg's unique culture. To

improve your vacation experience, observe customs and traditions where you are.

12. Stay adaptable: Finally, keep in mind that travel might be erratic. Be flexible with your plans and be open to new experiences. The most unforgettable experiences sometimes occur when you least expect them.

In conclusion, carefully considering a variety of aspects, such as your budget and travel plans, as well as your safety and cultural sensitivity, is necessary while organizing your excursion to Johannesburg. By making thorough plans ahead of time, you can make the most of this amazing city and create enduring experiences that will last with you long after your trip is over. Johannesburg welcomes the curious tourist with open arms and is prepared to reveal its delights.

Printed in Great Britain
by Amazon

29857793R00079